THE

OLIVE BRANCH;

OR,

THE EVIL AND THE REMEDY.

BY

CHARLES MINER.

PHILADELPHIA.
1856.

Printed by T K & P G Collins.

Dedicated,

WITH PROFOUND VENERATION AND RESPECT, TO

ROGER B. TANEY,

CHIEF-JUSTICE OF THE UNITED STATES,

AND

TO HIS ASSOCIATE JUSTICES,

BY

THE AUTHOR.

PREFACE.

The Introductory Address delivered at West Chester, Pennsylvania, at a celebration of the Declaration of Independence, July 4, 1821, immediately succeeding the excitement growing out of the admission of Missouri, is republished, to show the sentiments of the author then, which he has ever sincerely cherished, without variableness or shadow of turning, and as giving him some claim to a dispassionate hearing at the West and South on the delicate and exciting question of slavery.

He may be permitted to add, with pride, that the late venerated Chief-Justice Marshall caused the publication of the Address in a Richmond paper, with a commendatory introduction; and, among other numerous testimonials of approval, he received a flattering notice from the then President of Princeton College, to whom he was personally a stranger.

ADDRESS.

[After the seventh toast, the President called on Mr. Miner for a volunteer, who prefaced the sentiment by the following observations, which, by request, he has furnished for publication.]

Mr. President:—

I shall obey your call with pleasure; and, if it will not too much interrupt the flow of hilarity which prevails, I will offer you some reasons for the sentiment which I give.

It cannot have escaped you, that, in the discussions growing out of the Missouri controversy, a dissolution of the Union has been adverted to by zealous partisans on both sides of the question.

I confess to you, sir, that I cannot hear this subject spoken of without feelings of horror and dismay.

It sounds in my ear like a proposition of fratricide. Such a measure, it is manifest, could not be effected without the most desolating civil wars; and, should it be accomplished, would be followed by eternal contests between the neighboring tribes, (for they would no longer deserve the name of states or nations.) Standing armies, oppressive taxes, the violation of public rights and private security, and, finally, the subjugation of the whole by some military adventurer, would be the inevitable result.

I tremble to look down this dark abyss of misery and ruin. Despotism throughout the earth would exult at the issue, while wise and patriotic men, to the latest generations, would hold our name in pity and in scorn.

I do not make these remarks because I apprehend that on any side there is a disposition deliberately to bring about a separation. The man who should propose it would be driven by public indignation from society.

But rash and ambitious men, in moments of great excitement, inflamed by passion and reckless of consequences, may hereafter attempt the measure if the minds of the people are not effectually guarded against it.

The union of the States should be considered like freedom of conscience or the right of self-defence,—not for a moment to be brought in question.

The law of our union should be impressed upon our children as of the most sacred and paramount obligation. Habit is more powerful than law. Sentiment is more operative than reason.

I think, therefore, that law and reason should be fortified by habit and sentiment; and the doctrine should be inculcated in our schools, from the press, and in our public assemblies, so that successive generations may grow up with the impression indelibly fixed in their minds that the union of the States is the fundamental law on which our freedom is based, and the only sure foundation of our prosperity and glory.

I shall not attempt formally to reason this

matter, but I beg leave to repeat to you an old story:—

An Indian sachem, finding his life drawing to a close, called his children around him, and, holding out a bundle of rods bound firmly together, told his sons to break them. Each tried in his turn, but was unable. He then separated them, and broke each rod himself with ease. "Thus," said he, "will it be with you, my children. In union you will find safety; divided, your enemies will easily overpower you. These rods, firmly united, the efforts of strong men could not break; but, when separated, a feeble old man could destroy them."

After the late collision, in which we differed so widely and so warmly from our Southern friends, it may possibly be thought that something of prejudice against them may remain in our breasts.

Throughout Pennsylvania, I am bold to say that, whatever difference of opinion may exist on some subjects, there is no other general sentiment prevailing toward them than that of entire good will.

We are not only bound to the South by cords of interest, but by the stronger ties of affection. We not only find a satisfaction in the productiveness of her rice, sugar, cotton, and tobacco plantations, which contribute so largely to the national resources, but we participate in the pride of her chivalric character and exult in the triumphs of her eloquence and her arms. Her history and the fame of her heroes are the objects of our respect and veneration. The Southern are a high-spirited, mercurial people, distinguished by quickness of perception, rapidity of thought, and celerity of movement. Nice in their notions of honor, jealous of their rights, quick as lightning they flash when in collision; but, like the flint, they show a hasty spark, and straight are cold again. Withal they are frank, generous, brave, and hospitable, and, in truth, combine within themselves all the elements of a noble character.

Their fathers and our fathers fought many a well-contested field, side by side, for independence. Our Wayne and the gallant soldiers of the Pennsylvania line gathered laurels, which shall be ever green, in the same bloody conflicts which immortalized Monroe, Lee, Morgan, Pickens, Campbell, Pinckney, Sumpter, and Marion.

And what Pennsylvanian—nay, what American—is not proud to claim Laurens as his countryman? What bosom so cold as not to throb with rapture when the historian portrays the eloquence of Henry and of Randolph? American literature exhibits, with conscious pride, the works of Ramsey, Marshall, and of Wirt. And while older nations boast of their heroes and statesmen, we may point to a phalanx in Virginia, with Washington at their head, and boldly challenge a competition.

Southern statesmen, soldiers, and orators crowd so fast on the recollection that it is impossible to name them; but their fame is our common inheritance. And while the memorials of our nation shall endure, it will not be forgotten that at Yorktown, in Virginia, Cornwallis surrendered a numerous and well-appointed army to Washington and his comrades in arms; or that at New-Orleans Pakenham and his vaunted veterans were signally overthrown by Jackson and his gallant followers, our brethren of the West and South.

As the result of these views, I beg leave to give you

> "The United States and the citizens of the South. May our Union be everlasting as our hills, and may mutual good-will, freedom, and prosperity, like our rivers, flow through the land in perpetual streams."

Deeply impressed with the magnitude of the subject, I approach the practical point aimed at (in these letters) with all the solemnity of feeling its importance is calculated to inspire.

It has for many years occupied my most anxious thoughts,—sometimes the prospect gilded by hope, and not unfrequently overcast by clouds darkening to the hue of despair.

The voice of history audibly on every page tells us of and repeats to us the dire calamities of civil war; the inveterateness of hatred between those who, once friends, had become enemies; the excitability of the human temperament to deeds of retaliation and vengeance for real or imagined wrongs.

I am among those who apprehend, with inexpressible dread, that the dismemberment of this Union would give a death-blow to the last hope of

2

man's maintaining a government formed on the basis of justice, liberty, and equality,—where citizens of all religious persuasions, sects, or denominations, and of every shade of political opinion and creed, obedient to the laws, might enjoy the utmost freedom consistent with the freedom of their fellows, each family sitting under its own vine and fig-tree, with none to molest or make them afraid.

Treating of the vexed question of slavery, it is but just to myself, and respectful to the public, that I should declare what have been and are my sentiments upon the subject.

I hold that slavery is recognised by the Constitution. That there are certain concessions made to it in that instrument inalienably obligatory, except with the consent of the States where it exists. That slavery can have a being only by local law, and within the limits of the States where it is established; but, being at variance with natural law, that it cannot be established *de novo* anywhere, and can have no existence, rightfully, where it does not now prevail. That within those States neither the General Government, nor the other State Governments, nor individuals, have any right to interfere any more than with any other of their strictly municipal or social regulations. That, at the time of framing the Constitution, slavery was universally regarded as an evil present existing, to be kept within well-understood bounds. That, within the territories and all places under the jurisdiction of the general government, absolute power exists over it in Congress, accompanied with a duty, springing from the principles of eternal and unchangeable justice and the demands of sound policy, to abolish it and to prevent its extension. That the three-fifths rule, admitting the representation for slaves, is in the bond; and, however onerous now regarded, not to be disturbed, as I would not shatter a china vase because a speck on the enamel defaced its beauty. That the rendition of "persons held to service" escaping, being in the bond, ought to be fulfilled, but in a manner not to shock the moral sensibilities of the community.

I am free to confess that the experiment of the Fugitive Slave Law,—to which, in a moment of alarm, (and I regret it,) I gave my assent,—the frequent inhuman manner of its enforcement, wringing the heart with anguish,—the scenes in Boston and elsewhere,—the new doctrines since avowed, springing out of the concession,—fill my mind with apprehension. The repeal of the Missouri Compromise, the irritating and most exceptionable conduct of certain members of Congress while on its passage,—a repeal which any person predicting five years before would have subjected him to be denounced as an idiot, an incendiary, or a madman,—the unexampled outrages in Kansas, and the growing excitements in all parts of the Union, (sounding like the moan of the storm-demon along the base of the mountains,) —lead me to believe that a crisis has arrived when the slave-question must be met—met on both sides by the sober-minded, the wise, the prudent, the true conservative friends of the Constitution, the friends of this glorious Union, and of the great principles of religious and civil liberty contended for by our fathers.

Look at Mexico; run your eye over all South America; turn to Africa; scan Asia; examine Europe: is there aught in the whole vast scope of vision to lead one sensible and good man to desire an exchange, but rather to deprecate, curb, and restrain every rash footstep that would lead to revolution, anarchy, and civil war? In the midst of a stormy ocean, shall we break the ship in pieces, each of the crew depending upon a chance plank for safety when the sea is covered with wrecks?

One step farther at Boston, and a platoon of regular soldiers might have poured a volley of death into the crowded street; and who so prescient as to aver that civil war, in all its horrors, may not have ensued? An obscure smith, avenging the insult of a tax-gatherer to his daughter, set all England in a blaze. The "king, who was determined to try it," and his prime minister, North, had, or thought they had, law on their side, and were persuaded, we are to suppose, they were right. And so were those persuaded who had direction of the military when Burns was arrested. But the Adamses, Hancock, Warren, and others, differed from the king; and thousands of patriots, pure as they, with equally honest convictions, believe the recent measures in train equally despotic in their present aspect, and deem them not less fraught with danger to freedom and all that can make life desirable.

When Stringfellow attempted to throttle and chastise Governor Reeder, if equally-excited friends had rushed in to his rescue, who so wise in foresight as to aver that civil war would not then have ensued?

It seems to me we are marching over a magazine of powder, above which is erected a temple surpassing in beauty and exceeding in splendor that famed one of Ephesus, and which, I should fondly hope, in all our land there is no Eratostratus base enough willingly to set fire to, yet that is liable to be exploded by the passionate or thoughtless rashness of excited and inconsiderate partisans on either side. The recent event at South Carolina College, in Columbia, is a melancholy exemplification of the bewildering power of excited passion in uncorrupted youth, learned, polished in manners, and, when free from excitement, amiable to endearment, moving in the elevated walks of refined society.

The opinion formerly entertained, that slavery was an element of weakness, I am aware is discarded, and that it is now regarded as a power of great potency, capable of almost instant aggregation and discipline, by means of which the North may be governed at will.

A gentleman holding slaves, of high worth and habitually amiable deportment, said, in the presence of the writer, in a free discussion of the matter, in reply to a remark by a Northern man "that slaves rendered the South comparatively weak," "How mistaken! So far otherwise," said he, not vauntingly, but as expressing his clear convictions, "you lie at our mercy. These fellows, taught to seize a mad horse by the head, know nothing but obedience. We could place an army in the field before you could begin the slow process of rallying your militia." From the Rev. Mr. Breckenridge's letter it seems manifest he entertains the same opinion. It may be so. I hope the experiment may never be tried.

With the terror excited by the Southampton attempt at insurrection; with the scenes of St. Domingo fresh in recollection, few who reflect and are cautious in expressing their opinions, I think, will say "there is *no* domestic danger."

For my single self, I confess the principal cause of fear is in an

INVADING FOREIGN ENEMY.

An army of 150,000 men, 20,000 of them black regiments, trained and disciplined in the West Indies, all arrayed with revolt-inciting "banners," would be indeed "terrible." Those who look at the atrocities of the French revolution while Robespierre and Danton ruled,—or the barbarities of the French in the war of 1756, when the savages, armed with tomahawk and scalping-knife by that refined nation, were set ferociously on our defenceless frontiers,—or the blood-freezing enormities of the civilized Briton, playing the same death-march to the slaughter of unresisting innocence, with variations of increased cruelty, so late as the war of the Revolution,—can hardly affect to doubt that if interest, or passion, or policy, instigated the measure, they, either one or both combined, would renew the like sanguinary and cruel conflicts with the aid of their African allies.

All this appears too horrible to be thought of. To speak of it seems almost like treason. "Are they dogs, that they should do this thing?" And yet what are they now doing? Where are the legions of France and England at this hour, and what, in the name of heaven and humanity, are they about? How many lives have they already sacrificed of their own and the Russians, on the cold, lifeless pretence of policy, to preserve the balance of power, forsooth, which oceans of blood have never yet been able to establish!

If it be a possible—nay, more, a probable—danger, would it not be folly allied to weakness not to take early, instant, effective measures to disarm it?

A remark presses to my pen:—It is sometimes asked, "What has the North to do with slavery?" We answer, "It has to do with the already great and growing slave representation and its rapidly approaching overshadowing influence in the Senate and the General Government." The militia of the North, every man of them, are constitutionally bound to march at the call of the President to Georgia, Louisiana, Texas, or elsewhere, to put down an insurrection of slaves.

Nor is the danger to be disregarded arising from

the increasing mulatto, quadroon, and mustee population accumulating in the South,—many of them free, and a portion, not inconsiderable, partially educated, while some are even versed in classical literature and proficients in scientific attainments. On all these, however fair in complexion, polished in manners, or refined in taste, the ban of social outlawry is irrevocably passed. Their depression in the social scale, instead of humbling the mind to passive acquiescence in their doomed position, must kindle into intensest activity the spirit of ambition, while bitterest hatred, smothered under assumed respect, gathers daily strength in the proud breast which pants for an opportunity to revenge. With astonishing inconsistency, as it appears to me, and lack of foresight, the South is breeding and bringing up precisely the sort of men to take the initiative in an attempt at revolution and to lead in the field of battle, while superabundant materials of strong arms and willing hearts, it is manifest to a distant observer, lie amply before and all around them. Is it not natural to suppose "I bide my time" is the whisper of multitudes of those ostracized—the neither white nor black, neither citizens nor slaves? If not, all the teachings of history, of reason and experience, are false.

The powder is scattered far and wide — the seeds of threatening destruction. Accident, the self-igniting slow-match, time and chance, all, unforeseen, may light the torch. Then will be the call for a leader,— how important a material to success in any enterprise is manifest from the records of earliest time. It has grown into an apothegm that "deer led by a lion are more to be dreaded than lions led by a deer." What were the armies of Macedon without Alexander? of the Eastern Empire without Belisarius? of France without Napoleon? of England, in the Peninsular campaign, without Wellington?

And what statesman is there, North or South, the calibre of whose mind could carry his thoughts beyond the engrossing questions that occupy the buzzing insect-politicians that feed and fatten on the public offal,—whether John Doe or Richard Roe should occupy the White House or be sent minister to England,—that is not fully aware of the well-disciplined companies and regiments of blacks that parade, march, and countermarch, in the West India Islands and elsewhere, prepared and destined, in case of a desperate struggle and vengeful war, to find employment in checking the rising glories and humbling the proud boast of this envied, dreaded, and therefore hated, republic?

Regarding the danger certain, more or less remote, so also do I consider a preventive or remedy imperiously demanded by the "common welfare."

Who shall propose it?

Shall each one, waiting for another, sit down in silence and despair until the number of slaves has swelled to the portentous amount of ten millions? How long, even with the present decennial ratio of increase, before there might be counted *a million able to bear arms?*

The thought is appalling!

There is another source of danger, too probable and important to be omitted. I refer to that which might arise from famine. The extreme South, depending mainly on their cotton and sugar crops, seems specially exposed to the danger of want of food for their laborers. A frost, (the extreme severity of the passing winter, bearing its icy terrors far into Southern plains hitherto deemed beyond the reach of danger, cannot fail, methinks, to awaken inquietude in many a manly breast little accustomed to fear,) the rot, the army-worm, in multitudes, like the swarming grasshoppers that are spreading desolation all over Oregon and Utah, would assuredly be attended with distress to all, and possibly entail extreme suffering upon the more numerous dependent class, who have, it is supposed, neither the means nor the prospective care to provide for the supposed contingency. The suffering in Ireland from the loss of the potato-crop,—the continued distress in Madeira from the grape-failure,— the entire loss of the wheat-crop in extensive districts in New York and some Western States, which may become general, arising from the sudden advent of a mere tiny yellow fly, —all tend to show by what an "attenuated thread" we hold the means of life. "Hunger," says the old proverb, "will break through stone walls;" while every possible effort would be made by their masters, both from humanity and interest, to obtain relief for laborers. Yet, suffering themselves, their accustomed income cut off, it seems evident the evil might become so intense—as in European cities in time of scarcity—as to break down all the mounds of authority; and, the dykes once broken, who could stay the inundation?

Is the danger absolutely fanciful, indicated in the Virginia debates, that a portion of this Union may, by an unwise policy and an untoward series of events, become a great negrodom empire,—a sable despotism like Hayti,—the terror of all around them?

My proposition, submitted with all due deference, is this:—

That one hundred millions of dollars be appropriated for the gradual but certain extinguishment of slavery in the seven States named, to wit:—

Delaware,	Maryland,
Virginia,	Kentucky,
Tennessee,	Missouri,

Arkansas.

The public revenue is, happily, abundant. The fact has been again and again stated—and I do not learn that any man affects to doubt it—that our government authorized the offer of *one hundred and fifty millions* of dollars to purchase Cuba.

Now, I assume that, instead of augmenting the number of slaves and slave States, it would be wiser to lessen both, if it can be fairly accomplished with the consent of those principally interested.

I cast about for some ground of division that should be satisfactory, and come to the conclusion that as, in constituting Congress, (Senate and House,) a federal and popular combined basis had worked well, I would introduce it here. Multiply the whole number of slaves in those States by sixty,—to wit: 1,150,058 × 60 = 69,003,480, which, divided by the number in each State, would give each, on the popular basis, as follows:—

Delaware	132,000
Maryland	5,422,000
Virginia	28,351,680
Kentucky	12,658,860
Tennessee	18,367,540
Missouri	5,245,320
Arkansas	2,826,000
	69,003,480
Leaving a balance of	30,996,520
	100,000,000

Now the federal number, as must be obvious, is found by dividing that balance by seven:—

7) 30,996,520 (4,428,074.

Hence, Delaware would receive	132,000	
	4,428,074	4,560,074
Maryland...........................	5,422,080	
	4,428,074	9,850,154
Virginia	28,351,680	
	4,428,074	32,779,754
Kentucky	12,658,860	
	4,428,074	17,086,934
Tennessee.........................	14,367,540	
	4,428,074	18,795,614
Missouri	5,245,320	
	4,428,074	9,673.394
Arkansas.........................	2,826,000	
	4,428,074	7,254,074
		100,000,000

For this sum it is proposed a stock be issued by the General Government of fifty millions of dollars, bearing an interest of five per cent., payable semi-annually, irredeemable for twenty years. A further stock of fifty millions, bearing an interest for the first five years of two per cent., the second five years of three per cent., the third five years of four per cent., and thereafter five per cent., redeemable at pleasure.

To be delivered respectively to the States, or either of them which shall pass laws, in the nature of irrevocable contracts with the Federal Government, that no person born on or after the fourth of July, 1876, shall be a slave; and that after that day slavery shall cease to exist within the limits of the same, respectively.

And what would be the consequence? The stock so appropriated would be felt throughout this whole community of States only in its beneficence, in the confidence and harmony it would create and restore. It would bless those that give and those that take. In the States receiving it there would be no sudden disruption of existing ties. Business would flow on in its accustomed channels, only stimulated into greater healthful activity by abundant means. As the

Middle and Eastern States rose rapidly into opulence from the increased activity given to trade and industry by the capital distributed among them of Federal stock, under the funding system.

Twenty years, (the time allotted by the Constitution to terminate the slave-trade,) though it may seem long in a man's life, is yet a brief period in that of a nation.

The certainty that slavery would cease to exist in these States would lead thousands and tens of thousands of wholesome, moral, intelligent emigrants to hasten thither to a more southern aspect and genial clime,—

> "Where summer first unfolds her robes,
> And where she longest tarries,"

hastening to partake of the productive soil, the lovely climate, long the object of envy and desire, but which mothers were reluctant to remove to when their children must be brought up amid the degraded African race.

Lands—cultivated farms, or wild—rising in value to an amount enriching each State fourfold more than the stock received.

Railroads, schools, colleges, manufactories, mills, science, arts, education, every thing desirable to improve and adorn life, would receive an immediate and healthful impetus, quickened by the inspiring influence of assured freedom.

Let it be borne in mind that this plan of compromise is founded on the principle suggested in Mr. King's proposition in the Senate:—

"The interposition of the Federal Government, and the application of public lands to accomplish the end; thus substituting stock in money instead of land." Approved by the distinguished Virginian, Mr. Brodnax.

And, in regard to the *post nati*, justified by that eminent statesman, Mr. Rives. And that "*something should be done*," concurred in by the whole State of Virginia. Again and again it is pressed on every intelligent citizen, who desires to comprehend the actual state of the case, to read the proceedings and debates in the Virginia Assembly immediately subsequent to the Southampton insurrection.

O Virginia! Virginia! charming Virginia! It

would require the imagination of a poet to paint the instant and progressive advance which would render perfect the wishes and hopes of thy noble sons, whose fathers have gone down to the grave darkling almost in despair, knowing the evil, but seeing no remedy. Arise! Like Paul, shake the benumbing viper from your hand! You have but to *will* it, and you are free, prosperous, and soon again to be foremost in the rank of States.

Accompanying this great and healing measure, equally desirable to us and more important than the union of England and Scotland to them, should be the immediate repeal of the Fugitive Slave Law, so painfully, so dangerously irritating. But, as the Federal Government is bound to see that the Constitutional injunction be carried into effect, an arrangement should be made that a person escaping should be reclaimed as fugitives from justice now are,—by the application of the Governor of the State whence he fled to that of the State that harbors him; and, on failure of being delivered up, the General Government should pay to the claimant one-half, or something more, of his assessed value, the amount to be charged to the State so failing; the matter to be adjusted in the final settlement of accounts between them.

Slavery confined to those States whose productions of cotton, rice, and sugar are supposed to require their labor, all danger to them from within or without would cease, and the utmost degree of prosperity they are capable of would ensue.

Receiving from the seven States who were in a gradual train of winding up their concern with them, the cotton and sugar plantations would be supplied on moderate terms, and there could be no motive hence to urge the reopening of the slave-trade in the annexation of Cuba.

The jarring notes of discord throughout the land would cease, so desirable everywhere, not least desirable among our Christian friends.

There are fifteen million persons in the free States. The sum to be paid, even if assessed on them, would not come to seven dollars each,—not thirty-five cents a year. The revenue from imported silks alone would pay the interest and redeem the stock within the twenty years.

An important consideration remains to be noted. The power and application of steam have brought Africa to our doors.

There should forthwith, from two to four—more if necessary—large steamers be placed by Government at the disposal of the Colonization Society; five per cent., more or less, should be reserved, to be expended by the Colonization Society under the supervision of the President; the healthful highlands of Africa should be explored and purchased, the colored race be aided *home,* encouraged, defended; while their commerce would, like the full breasts of the Roman daughter, return to our merchants a revenue ample to repay every expense incurred. Civilization, knowledge, Christianity, would go in their train; and that fine country, so susceptible of improvement, so long a "Paradise lost," would, under Providence, by our and their instrumentality, become a "Paradise regained."

Oh, what a glorious theme!

Oh, from the sacred altar, "a coal like that which touched Isaiah's hallowed lips with fire," to kindle the eloquence of our clergy everywhere, and of every denomination, to plead for it.

All which is respectfully submitted by

CHARLES MINER.

WILKES-BARRÉ, *Pa., March* 17, 1856.

THE END.

www.ingramcontent.com/pod-product-compliance
Lightning Source LLC
LaVergne TN
LVHW011123110826
845150LV00008B/2237